To Dylan

Robert Edward Gurney

ISBN 978-0-9928690-3-8

Published in the United Kingdom in 2014 by
Cambria Books, Wales, United Kingdom

Poet's Introduction

It is the sound of Dylan's voice, the sound of his poetry read aloud, either by Dylan himself, many years ago, on the BBC or by another Welsh person, by Anthony Hopkins, by Richard Burton, or by a friend of mine, the late Philip Madoc, that has inspired me. When I write a poem I often hear Dylan's voice in my head. It is sonorous, baritone, deep and it echoes in the mind.

A poem in which I heard Dylan's voice or, if you like, that I wrote with Dylan's voice seemingly articulating the words in my head, was 'Sounds'. It describes the sounds of my home town that I heard when I was growing up. I dispense with punctuation in much of the poem as the sounds drift in and out of my memory.

As I often hear or imagine Dylan's voice when I am writing, I also often imagine Dylan doing something or other. I see him debating with his friends in the Kardomah (both the old and the new) in Swansea, for example ('The Toddington Poetry Society', 'The Kardomah').

A gentleman, the JP in one of the Kardomah poems, who lives on a farm to the north of Swansea in a place called Cwmgwili, said to me of Poetry some ten years ago: "It flows though the air" [in Wales]. I tend to think that it flows through the air in many places, not all, but it is true that it is almost tangible in Wales.

To my wife Paddy

THE POEMS

The White Lady

to Ketty Lis

The night was as black as a bible.

We were driving down a lane in Wales

when I thought that I almost saw her in my headlights

the white lady

sitting on a gate.

I didn't know who she was

or what she meant.

She seemed to be mourning

the theft of the stone circle

from the field behind her.

Then I thought I saw Dylan
shuffling towards a village
in search of cigarettes from a machine that was
broken.

Then a barn owl with white wings
as broad as my car
attracted by my lights
swooped down, nearly smashing the windscreen.
I stopped
there was nothing.

I don't know what this means
but I can intuit it.

A friend of mine, who lives in Rosario,
says the white lady is poetry.

I remember having seen her

once

in a poem by Rimbaud

about a waterfall.

I must look for the book by Robert Graves

about this.

The Photograph

I sat down
on the beach
in Port Eynon.

I put the photograph down
on the sand.

It was of a friend
and his father
by a lake.

I thought of Dylan
and his father
and of me and mine.

I fell asleep.

When I woke up
the tide had come in
and the photo
was disappearing
beneath the water.

The Heron

There is a heron
in a pool
at the side of the road
that crosses
the empty plain
in Gower.

It doesn't see Dylan
passing by,
climbing Cefn Bryn.

The Crows

The inhabitants of Port Eynon
have a nickname,
they are called the crows.

There are some tall, scrawny fir trees
on the cliff above our house
full of crows that fly up
into the teeth of the wind.

They call out over The Ship
where Dylan drank
and watched them through the portholes
planning a night of passion.

Their caws are dark stains
on the transparent air
that whips the village.

Sitting by the fire
we can hear their cries
coming down the chimney.

They make us think of Vincent
and the temptation to brave the elements.

Words on Water

I dreamt last night
of somebody.

I think it was Dylan.

He had a fishing net in his hand
like the ones children sometimes use
to catch butterflies.

The words
"Rage, rage, against the dying of the light".
and "Do not go gentle into that good night",
were floating down
the slow-flowing stream.

I think it was Dylan
but it may have been Francis Bacon,
or me as a child,

or even me now,
 - I can't remember -
squatting there by the water,
catching the letters
and putting them in a pile
next to me
on the river bank
higgledy-piggledy.

The Da Vinci Code

On the cliffs
in the distance
above the village
of Horton
huge cows
magnified
by a trick of the light
are eating the grass.

On the beach below
the trees
in Port Eynon Bay
where Dylan once sat
beautiful women in bikinis
are reading a book
that some say
is full of lies.

Dylan's Bay

I rang the monumental mason
on my mobile
to discuss the words
for my mother-in-law's tomb.

He said he was working
in the most beautiful spot
in the world,
overlooking Swansea Bay.

He was, he said,
in Oystermouth Cemetery,
not far from Dylan's house.

The Shepherd

I used to see him
tending his sheep
in a field
above Port Eynon.

We would talk
about Dylan.

He told me with pride
that he had preached in Welsh
at the funeral of a friend
in the Church of Saint Catwgg.

Then he said
that someone had asked him
afterwards
why the devil he had used
that 'foreign' language.

A few months later
they found him in his house
at the top of the cliff
hanging by the neck.

The Mist

to Thomas Gray (1716-1771)
and Vernon Watkins (1906-1967)

The sea-mist rolls in
obliterating the landscape.

The first to go is the sea,
then sand dunes as big as pyramids.

It creeps up the road
erasing The Captain's Table
and The Ship
where Dylan once drank.

The tree tops disappear,
then the cliffs.

All that is left
are some marks in the sky,
the crows that are hovering
without moving.

And through the mist can be heard
as clear as the church bell
the sad tolling of the buoy
in Overton Mere.

Dylan at Play

It's strange
to think
that Dylan
used to walk up and down the river bank
and play in the hay
behind the Kingsbridge Inn,
the Tafarn-y-Trap pub
and Ken Pollard's Dance School
in Gorseinon,
here, on the flood plain,
where they are building
a village of expensive houses.

The Toddington Poetry Society

I was sitting
in The Kardomah,
Dylan's old coffee bar
in Swansea,
trying to imagine him
and his friends
around me.

I had also gone,
I must admit,
to see if I had remembered
the Chinese man in the window
correctly.

I felt a bit bad
when I saw
that the tea chests
he was carrying
were bigger than I thought

and the grimace on his face
was less obvious.

I sat down
opposite a gentleman
who turned out to be
a JP.

"Ah, the Kardomah boys",
he said,
when I told him why
I was there.

I said
that I was preparing a poem
for the Toddington
Poetry Society.

"What a beautiful name",
he sighed,
to my surprise,
"Tod-ding-ton".

The Kardomah

I went there again today
to that long window
of the Kardomah
behind Marks and Spencer.

The place was full of Americans
asking about Dylan

I could have sworn
I heard Dan Jones saying
that he was going to compose
a great symphony

and Dan Janes proclaiming
that he would paint
the perfect picture

and Charlie Fisher boasting
that he would catch
the biggest trout

and Vernon and Dylan announcing
they would write
the greatest poems.

The Chinese Worker

I couldn't sleep
last night.

I was translating
China 8 mm
by Andrés Bohoslavsky

In the darkroom
of my mind
a butterfly was flapping
at the window
trying to get out.

A poem
began to appear.

I see the Chinese man
that fills
the window
of the Kardomah
in Swansea
where, I was told,
Dylan met his friends.

It's a statue of a man
carrying a pole
on his shoulders
on either end of which
hang baskets of tea.

He is wearing a conical
Chinese hat
and Chinese clothes.

His face is screwed up
with the effort
although, to be honest,
the tea doesn't look that heavy

Behind him
I am sure I can see Dylan
through the glass
and his friends,
Charlie Fisher and Daniel Jones,
Fred Janes and Thomas Warner,
and Vernon Watkins
arguing about poetry
and painting,
music and politics,
Einstein and Epstein,
ambition and Stravinsky
death and religion,
Garbo and Picasso,
and girls

free beer and free love,
Communism and Symbolism,
Bradman and Braque,
Michelangelo and murder,
ping-pong and Sibelius,
anarchy and darts,
and girls

Augustus John and Dracula,
the Welsh sea and the London stars,
trial marriage and T. S Eliot,
Amy Johnson and King Kong,
and girls.

I could hear the hiss
of their cigarette butts
in the bottom
of their coffee cups.

I know I could have met them,
some of them at least,
but I didn't.

"Look", whispered an old painter,
"It wasn't here that we met.
It was in the old Kardomah in Castle Street,
the one that was flattened by the bombing."

The Harlequin

I went to look for
a coffee bar
in Luton yesterday.

I could hear us talking
so many years ago.

One was saying
he would conduct
a great orchestra

another that he would launch
the Reality Party

another that he would become
a jazz musician.

I heard myself saying
that I would write
a novel.

I look for the stairs
and the paintings
of figures from the circus
who were flying and dancing
on the walls
but they were no longer there.

There's just a wall there now
where the entrance used to be.

Sounds

I remember
the sound
of the Town Hall Clock.

On a good day
you could hear it
a couple of miles away.

The town
was full
of sounds:

the rooks
in Lovers' Lane

the news vendor
on the corner
opposite The Brewery Tap

who did bird whistles
while waiting to sell
the next paper

the sirens
warning
of an impending
attack

tea break time at Vauxhall
announced by a fanfare
of trumpets

then the chimes
to say that the break
was over

in the fifties
and sixties
you had to put your hands
over your ears
when the wind tunnel started up
at the airport

(there was talk
of secret missiles)

the hum
of the MI
in the distance

the chimes of the Westminster clock
that sat on our mantle-piece
imitating Big Ben
and which I haven't rewound
since my parents died.

Prize Giving

She is standing there
by the lake
in Verulamium Park
dressed like the moon
in a poem by Lorca,
a straw hat
and a long mauve robe
down to the ground.

Hundreds of birds
rush towards her.

Mallards,
Canadian geese
and moorhens
streak across the water.

Seagulls swoop.

There are exotic birds
whose names
I cannot remember
and a swan
with a broken wing.

Herons
cock mad eyes at her
from the heronry
in the weeping willows
on the island.

A duck,
its head stuck
in one of the plastic rings
of a four-pack,
swims round in circles.

She opens a bag
and throws
pieces of stale bread
onto the water.

The Lock-Up

There's a lock-up in Shenley
not far from London
between the pub and the pond.

It’s shaped like a fat bottle.

They have closed it now.

It's only there
for the tourists.

Each time that I passed it
on my way to St Albans
I saw myself staring out,
watching Dylan and Vincent
and one or two others
coming and going
as they pleased.

Port Eynon From Space

to Vicente Huidobro

The sun is setting.
The sky is cloudless.
The earth looks beautiful.
Half of it is in darkness.
Its cities are bright dots.
The lights are on
in Barcelona and Paris.
It is still daylight
in London and Madrid.
The sun is still shining
in Ceuta and Gibraltar.
It's night time
in the Mediterranean.
In the middle of the Atlantic
you can see the Azores.
Below them, to the right,
is Madeira

Further down are the Canaries.
Close to Africa,
you can see Cape Verde Islands.
The Sahara is huge
and can be seen
even at night.
To the left, on top,
is Greenland,
totally frozen.
There's a flash of light in Port Eynon,
as I open the bedroom window
to let a butterfly out.
Did you see it, Vicente?

Dylan Down Here

I was tempted
to dedicate my poem
'Port Eynon From Space'
just to Dylan.

But I thought, somehow,
that it wouldn't be right.

I wanted to ask him
if he could see
how beautiful Gower looks
when seen from space.

But then I remembered
that Dylan used to tumble about
in the here and now,
in the undergrowth
below the cliff.

I am not sure
that he was ever up there
in space
with Vicente Huidobro.

He spent more time
down here, I think,
walking by the stream
that fed his uncle's mill
in Kingsbridge.

The Bonfire

Some years ago
I went to look
for some of Dylan's letters
in The Boathouse
that overlooks the sea
in Laugharne.

Somebody had told me
that he had hidden them
in the roof.

I spoke to the builder
who had been renovating
the building.

He said yes,
that he had found them,
together with some other papers,

but that they were all so dirty
that he had had to burn them
on a big bonfire
on the patio
next to the house.

The Pawn Shop

Beauty runs a Pawn Shop
and accepts just the hearts of men.
When the time comes to recover them
she has shut up shop.

Chu Siang (1904-1933)

I went looking
for the Pawn Shop
in Bute Street,
Luton,
to try to redeem
the manuscript
of some poems
about a love affair
that I left there
forty years ago.

The street
was no longer there.

In its place
they have built
an American-style
shopping mall.

Brown's

"By the way,"
I asked the barman
in Brown's, Dylan Thomas' pub,
in Laugharne,
"did the poet get drunk?"

"No," he said,
"he didn't.

He usually drank
half a pint
before going back
to the Boathouse
to write."

The King's Head

I looked in through the window
of 'The King's Head'
in Llangennith
and I thought that I saw Dylan
sitting on the stairs,
by himself,
with his head
in his hands.

Under Milk Wood

I was talking to a solicitor
who lives near Llareggub,
a man who looks after
the wills and deeds
of the rural aristocracy.

He shoots ducks.

I asked him what he thought
of Dylan Thomas

He answered
that he had just seen
Under Milk Wood
in the Grand Theatre in Swansea
and, frankly.
he had not liked it.

I don't know why,
something in his manner, perhaps,
but I didn't ask him why.

Dylan and Diana

I intended to visit yesterday
Diana's Fountain
in London.

I wanted to see
the fountain of life
that runs in a circle
in Hyde Park.

I wanted to dip my hand
in the calm parts of the water
in the turbulent, the beautiful, the disturbed,
in the fast and the slow.

I wanted to touch the marble.

I found myself instead
imagining Dylan,
standing there,
cracking jokes
in a bar in Soho.

The White Ladies of Carmarthen

He sat on the river bank
of the River Towey.

The night was psalter-black.

In the distance
he saw two boatloads of women
wearing white robes
crossing the river.

When the boats reached
the middle of the stream,
he saw in the moonlight
that they were coracles
and that when they reached
the other side,
the women inside them
had turned into black cats.

Infinity

to Arthur Rimbaud

Sitting high up
on the cliff
at Worm's Head,
I watch
the sun setting.

A red stain
is vanishing
behind a curtain of grey.

Little by little
the sea disappears.

The sea leaves
with the sun,
whispers Rimbaud.

The Witch

It was in a farmhouse
near 'The King's Head'
in Llangennith
in the far west of Gower.

A farmer who knew the dialect
had agreed to see me.

He's on his death bed,
people were saying.

It was pitch black,
there were no lights.

A shooting star streaked brightly
across the sky.

Will I be too late?
I asked myself,
as I let myself in.

He was alone.

A moth was fluttering
against his oil lamp.

“We call them witches,”
he whispered.

“Witches?” I repeated.

“Yes, witches,” he said.

“Moths come out at night.
Witches come out at night?”

“Yes,” he breathed.

"Moths undergo metamorphosis,
witches can transform themselves
into cats?"

"That's what some used to say,"
he murmured.

"Moths fly by night.
Witches fly by night?"

"Yes."

"Witches have long noses.
Moths have long noses?"

"Perhaps," he replied
with a faint smile.

"Do you believe in witches?" I asked.

"Don't be ridiculous!" he cried.

Arthur's Stone

I have heard it said
that, at full moon,
young women would crawl three times
around or under Arthur's Stone
where Dylan once sat.

They say they would place
an offering upon the stone:
a cake made with barley and honey
and wetted with milk.

It is said that they were testing
their lovers' fidelity
and that if he appeared
before they had finished
he would stay faithful for life.

I read somewhere else
that they just wanted
to get pregnant.

The Way We Are Now

You go down to Wales
to the house of your wife's parents
in the village by the sea
where people seem as large
as the characters in *Under Milk Wood*
where everyone knows everyone
and where they notice
if even a blade of grass
has been moved.

The sun and sea-bleached statue of Billy Gibbs,
the lifeboat man who died saving others,
is always there,
just by the Church of St Cattwg,
looking out over the bay
and at people who come and go.

You go down now and then,
in the school holidays,
with the children,
whenever you can.

You make friends with a German family
you never see again.

You strike up a friendship
with a Danish violinist
who never returns.

There was that French family who said
that it is better
than the south of France.
They didn't come back.

And there was that nice family
from South-East London
who now go now to a 'better' village
nearer to Rhossili.

But you feel at home.

Sometimes there is a gap,
something comes up
that stops you getting down.

The car's playing up.
A friend you haven't seen
for twenty years
is coming from Bilbao.

Someone you have never met
but with whom you exchange e-mails
is coming from Buenos Aires.

Someone falls ill.
You can't get away.

You stay at home.

And then you go back
and ask "How is old Myfanwy
from Mumbles?"

"Oh, didn't you know,
she died last winter,
aged ninety-two."

"And how is The Reverend Jenkins?"
"Oh, he died too."

"And what about The Captain
who was always in The Ship?"
"He passed away last summer."

"And Mrs Beynon?"
"She's gone too."

"And Mr Pugh in the big house?"
"He died in Malta."

"And Mr Ogmore
who cut the grass in the graveyard?"
"Gone."

They all had big funerals
and you just didn't know.

We were all once like that,
like those people in that village
under the cliff.

The Land of Poets

It was midnight.

25 degrees below zero.

The bus broke down
on the road between
Trelew to Esquel
in a place called
Plumas.

There were wild dogs
everywhere.

I thought I heard Dylan
whisper in my ear:

"This is a country
where they take poets
very seriously."

Rhossili

I had a message today
from Catamarca in Argentina.

In it my friend said
that she loved her mountains,
that they changed colour
according to the time of day
but that today
she could not see them
behind the clouds.

She had to imagine them.

She also seemed sad
that she didn't know
about an ancestor
called Heller.

I told her
that I knew a man
called Heller
who ran a hotel on top of the cliff
at Worm's Head
in Gower.

I told her how once
he opened the door
and shook his fist
at a hang glider pilot
who was hovering
too near his windows.

"You're banned",
he shouted.

Today he lies in the cemetery
of St Mary's Church
overlooking Rhossili Bay
the most beautiful bay,
in the world,

some locals say.

I think he knew Dylan.

It is easy to imagine it
once you have seen it.

Just close your eyes.

I can see myself
sitting next to Dylan,
sad,
on the cliff top,
looking out to sea.

My Son's Dream

to my son William

We were walking
through the waves
on the beach
in Port Eynon
without a care
in the world.

We didn't see it coming,
the tsunami.

We were pointing
at tall stones
that had been carved
into statues
standing in the water
some distance
from the shore.

One of them
looked like Dylan.

Then it hit us.

I was hurled
onto the rocks.

My brother
and his friend
were sucked out.

Everybody disappeared
but me,
under the waves.

I ran into the water
to try to rescue my brother
and his girl friend
but they were nowhere
to be seen.

One by one
people started bobbing up
gasping for air.

I had almost given up hope
when they reappeared
and threw themselves
on to the ground
on a mound
behind the Salt House.

Dicing With Death

To my cousin, Anne Allen

Do you remember, Dylan,
how the trains used to rush
through the station?

They seemed to suck you
towards the edge of the platform.

You felt
that if you stood too near
you would be gone for ever.

As youngsters we would play
solitary chicken,
standing too near
as the train hurtled past
almost invisibly,
like a giant bull,

with a loud 'olé',
disappearing
in a puff of smoke.

I can still see my cousin Anne,
the same age as me,
eleven,
standing there
beside the road
in Baglan,
like a black and white photograph of an angel,
a second before she was gone,
the car, the bumper, her dress,
a tiny black bruise on her forehead,
that’s all,
under her ash-blonde hair.

Some said we were like twins.

I still keep that photograph
in my head
and I still visit her grave
in Houghton Regis,
whenever I can.

A Post Card from Ushuaia

A tin roofed shelter
protects me from the wind
in this small bay
at the end of the world.

An old oil drum
serves as my barbecue.

The albatross
approaches my hand
to snatch and gulp down
voraciously
the pieces of meat
I offer it.

The lighthouse stares at me
red, white, red,
blankly.

The White Lady of Caswell Bay

They say
that a witch
fashions the sand
into castles
in Caswell Bay.

They say
that they can withstand
the movement
of the tides.

They say
that if you look closely
you can see
her invisible hands.

I am not so sure
that they are hers.

I like to think

that they belong

to someone else.

By the same author:

La poesía de Juan Larrea

Poemas a la Patagonia

Luton Poems

Nueve monedas para el barquero

El cuarto oscuro y otros poemas

La libélula y otros poemas / The Dragonfly and Other Poems

La casa de empeño y otros poemas / The Pawn Shop and Other Poems

A Night in Buganda: Tales from Post-Colonial Africa

Translation: The River and Other Poems (Andrés Bohoslavsky)

Orders: bob@verpress.com or verpress.com

www.ingramcontent.com/pod-product-compliance
Ingram Content Group UK Ltd.
Pitfield, Milton Keynes, MK11 3LW, UK
UKHW020236250726
13967UKWH00001B/402

9 780992 869038